919.89
Wh;

WITHDRAWN

Endurance

Shipwreck and Survival on a Sea of Ice

by Matt White

Reading Consultant:
Timothy Rasinski, Ph.D.
Professor of Reading Education
Kent State University

Capstone Curriculum Publishing

Capstone Curriculum Publishing materials are published by Capstone Press, P.O. Box 669, 151 Good Counsel Drive, Mankato, Minnesota, 56002 http://www.capstone-press.com

Copyright © 2002 Capstone Press. All rights reserved.

Library of Congress Cataloging-in-Publication Data
White, Matt, 1955-
    Endurance: shipwreck and survival on a sea of ice/by Matt White
    p. cm.
    Includes bibliographical references (p. 62).
    Summary: Tells the story of the shipwreck of the Endurance in a sea of ice en route to Antarctica, and the amazing survival of all 28 members of the Imperial Trans-Antarctic Expedition, led by Sir Ernest Shackleton.
    ISBN 0-7368-9500-0 (pbk.) - ISBN 0-7368-4000-1 (hardcover)
    1. Shackleton, Ernest Henry, Sir,
1874-1922—Journeys—Antarctica—Juvenile literature. 2. Endurance (Ship)—Juvenile literature. 3. Imperial Trans-Antarctic Expedition (1914-1917)—Juvenile literature. 4. Antarctica—Discovery and exploration—Juvenile literature. [1. Shackleton, Ernest Henry, Sir, 1874-1922—Journeys. 2. Endurance (Ship) 3. Imperial Trans-Antarctic Expedition (1914-1917) 4. Antarctica—Discovery and exploration.] I. Title.
G850 1914.S53 W55 2001
919.8904—dc21

                                        2001001981

Created by Kent Publishing Services, Inc.
Designed by Signature Design Group, Inc.

This publisher has made every effort to trace ownership of all copyrighted material and to secure necessary permissions. In the event of any questions arising as to the use of any material, the publisher, while expressing regret for any inadvertent error, will be happy to make necessary corrections.

Photo Credits:
Cover, Corbis/Bettmann; pages 4, 6, 12, 16, 18, 27, 32, 33, 35, 38, 41, 46-47, 48-49, 50-51, 54, 57, Royal Geographic Society, London; pages 11, 31, 42-43, 55, Scott Polar Research Institute; pages 20-21, 22, 26, 28-29, 36, Corbis/Bettmann

No part of this book may be reproduced without written permission from the publisher. The publisher takes no responsibility for the use of any of the materials or methods described in this book, nor for the products thereof.

Printed in the United States of America.

2 3 4 5 6 07 06 05 04 03 02

Table of Contents

Chapter 1: Locked in Ice 5

Chapter 2: Breaking Up 16

Chapter 3: Adrift 26

Chapter 4: Rescue Party 36

Chapter 5: Survivors 46

Epilogue 54

Time Line 58

Glossary 60

Bibliography 62

Useful Addresses 63

Internet Sites 63

Index 64

Locked in Ice

Imagine being shipwrecked on a sea of ice. There is no way to break free. The nearest help is 800 miles (1,287 kilometers) away. There is little shelter from the freezing cold. There is little to eat but penguins and seals. For 28 unlucky men aboard the ship Endurance, this really happened. Here is their story.

Setting Sail for Antarctica

In 1914, Sir Ernest Shackleton set sail for Antarctica on the ship *Endurance*. With him were a team of 26 men plus one stowaway.

Explorers had been to Antarctica before. But no explorer had crossed this frozen continent on foot. Shackleton wanted to be the first. He planned to walk from the Weddell Sea on one side of Antarctica to the Ross Sea on the other. This distance is about 1,800 miles (2,897 kilometers)!

---

stowaway: one who hides on a ship to ride for free
continent: any of the seven great land masses on Earth

The Men

Aboard *Endurance* were two teams. The ship's crew would navigate, steer, and do repairs on *Endurance*. The expedition members, mainly scientists, would record temperatures and weather. They would also study the land, ice, and any life forms. The surgeons would keep the men healthy. Also on board *Endurance* were 69 sled dogs and Mrs. Chippy, the carpenter's cat.

Team members of Endurance

navigate: to follow a course or direction using a map, compass, stars, or other tools
expedition: a group making a long trip for a special purpose

Endurance Crew and Expedition Members

Sir Ernest Shackleton . . . . Leader
Frank Wild . . . . Second-in-command
Frank Worsley . . . . Captain
Hubert Hudson . . . . Navigating officer
Lionel Greenstreet . . . . First officer
Thomas Crean . . . . Second officer
Alfred Cheetham . . . . Third officer
Louis Rickinson . . . . Chief engineer
A.J. Kerr . . . . Second engineer
Dr. Alexander Macklin . . . . Surgeon
Dr. James McIlroy . . . . Surgeon
James Wordie . . . . Geologist
Leonard Hussey . . . . Meteorologist
Reginald James . . . . Physicist
Robert Clark . . . . Biologist
James "Frank" Hurley . . . . . Official photographer
George Marston . . . . Official artist
Charles Green . . . . Cook
Harry McNeish . . . . .Carpenter
Walter How . . . . Able seaman
William Bakewell . . . . Able seaman
Timothy McCarthy . . . . Able seaman
Thomas McLeod . . . . Able seaman
John Vincent . . . . Able seaman
Ernest Holness . . . . Fireman
William Stevenson . . . . Fireman
Percy Blackborrow . . . . . . Stowaway, later steward
Thomas Orde-Lees . . . . Motor engineer
and storekeeper

7

South to the Ice

Endurance first sailed across the Atlantic Ocean to South America. From there, it went to South Georgia Island. This island sits in the Weddell Sea. South Georgia Island became the last point of human contact. It was also the last source of supplies.

Around Antarctica, the sea freezes into pack ice. Sailing in this area is dangerous. Ships can hit icebergs and sink. The ice can freeze around a ship, trapping and crushing it.

Endurance would face more than 1,000 miles (1,609 kilometers) of these risks just to get from South Georgia Island to the Antarctic coast. Then, the men would use dog sleds to cross Antarctica on foot.

---

pack ice: large, floating pieces of ice frozen together
iceberg: a large mass of ice floating in a sea

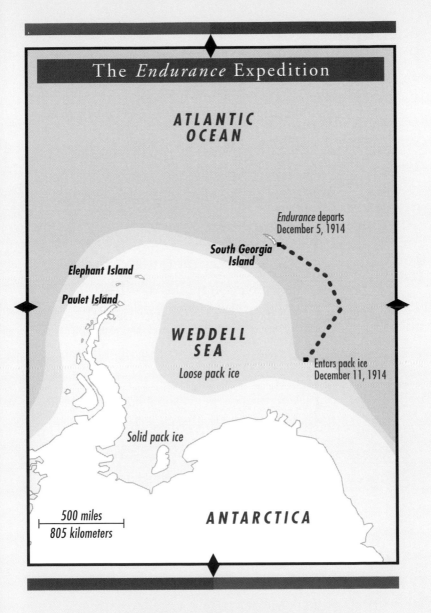

The *Endurance* Expedition

ATLANTIC
OCEAN

Endurance departs
December 5, 1914

**South Georgia
Island**

Elephant Island

Paulet Island

WEDDELL
SEA

Loose pack ice

Enters pack ice
December 11, 1914

Solid pack ice

500 miles
805 kilometers

ANTARCTICA

*Once the men on Endurance left South Georgia Island,
they were on their own sailing toward a sea of ice.*

Trapped

Endurance left South Georgia Island on December 5, 1914. By December 7, the Weddell Sea's floating ice surrounded her. But *Endurance*, a strong ship, broke her way through the ice. For a month, she was free. Then on January 18, 1915, thick pack ice stopped her completely.

That night, a cold gale blew up. It pressed ice close around the ship. By the next day, *Endurance* was trapped. Attempts to break the ice and free the ship failed.

Life on the Ice

Temperatures on the ice dipped to –30° Fahrenheit (–34° Celsius). The men played soccer to stay warm. At night, they slept in sleeping bags. The reindeer skin sleeping bags were warmest. The other bags were woolen. Everybody slept on board the ship. The sailors slept in the forecastle. Officers and scientists slept in the wardroom.

---

gale: a strong wind
forecastle: the front part of a ship's upper deck
wardroom: the officers' lounge

The dogs stayed on the ice beside *Endurance*. The men made igloos to keep the dogs warm. The sailors called these "dogloos." The men played regularly with these tough dogs. They thought of them as pets, not just working dogs.

The men made "dogloos" to keep the dogs warm.

igloo: a house made of ice

Keeping Busy

The scientists had planned to study rocks on Graham Land and Enderby Land. Now they couldn't do that work.

Instead, the scientists studied the Weddell Sea. They took soundings to measure the sea's depth. To do this, they dropped a lead weight on a rope into the sea. The rope was marked in fathoms. When the weight hit bottom, they recorded the depth.

The men played soccer for fun and to stay warm.

sounding: a measurement of depth
fathom: a unit of measure; 1 fathom = 6 feet or 1.8 meters

Danger Grows

The expedition was in trouble. Blizzards swept the area. *Endurance* sat frozen in the middle of an ice floe. These flat sheets of ice float on the ocean. Many miles wide, they move all the time. The ship slowly drifted north on the floe.

Everywhere the men looked was solid ice. The men did not feel as if they were moving. But they were. The ice floe drifted on the ocean currents, taking the ship with it.

What's more, the ice was drifting the wrong way. Already, *Endurance* had drifted north of Shackleton's planned landing point. Every day, they drifted farther from their goal.

Sometimes ice nearby *Endurance* cracked open. Then the men would try to cut a path to the open water. But the ice always closed up again. The ice floe took *Endurance* farther and farther north, away from land.

---

blizzard: a severe snowstorm
floe: a floating island of ice

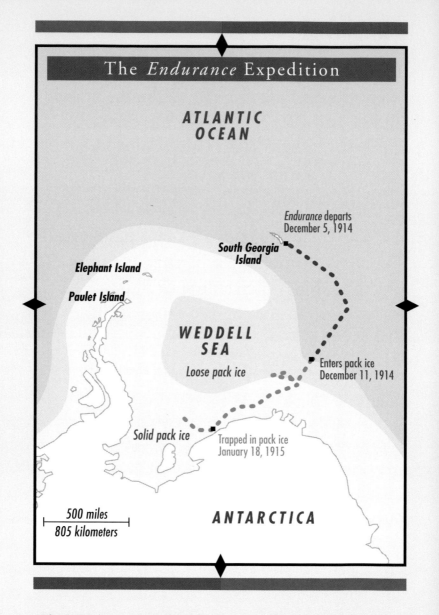

The *Endurance* Expedition

ATLANTIC
OCEAN

Endurance departs
December 5, 1914

**South Georgia
Island**

Elephant Island

Paulet Island

*WEDDELL
SEA*

Loose pack ice

Enters pack ice
December 11, 1914

Solid pack ice

Trapped in pack ice
January 18, 1915

500 miles
805 kilometers

ANTARCTICA

Thick pack ice stopped Endurance completely on January 18, 1915. The men were unable to free the ship from the solid ice.

Time to Leave?

Endurance could not last much longer. Ice would soon crush the ship if the men could not free it.

Shackleton faced some tough questions. Do they try to march across the ice floes to land? How long should they stay with the trapped ship? Will the men be able to free *Endurance* from her icy berth? Or will she be crushed in an icy embrace?

---

berth: a place where a boat is tied up
embrace: a hug

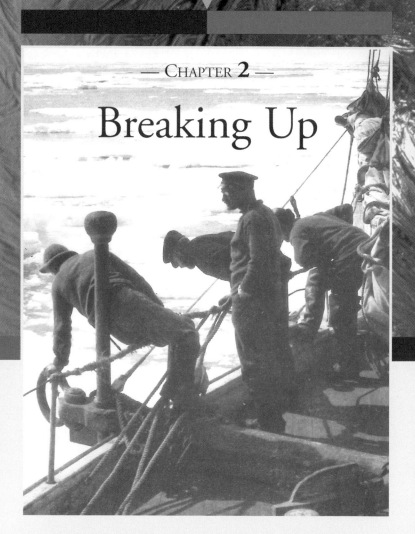

— CHAPTER **2** —

Breaking Up

*Sir Ernest Shackleton's expedition is in peril.
Endurance is trapped in ice. Will the ice break
and let Endurance go free? What will the men
do if the ship is crushed? Can they survive?*

peril: danger

A Strong Ship

Endurance was a wooden ship made to sail in icy waters. Built in Norway, she had a strong bow. *Endurance* could take bumps from ice.

Some ships built to sail in icy waters have curved sides. When such a ship gets caught in ice, the pressure will push the ship up on top of the ice. *Endurance* did not have curved sides. She had a flat-sided hull. This is why she became trapped.

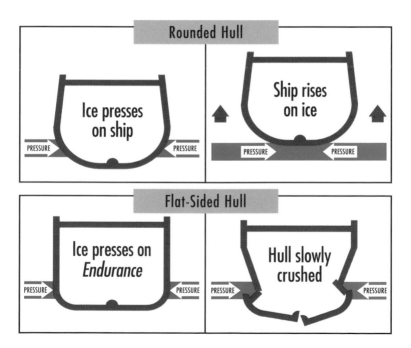

bow: the front of a ship
hull: the frame or body of a ship

Not Strong Enough

When water freezes, it expands. The ice of a frozen sea can easily crush a ship. *Endurance* withstood the ice from January until late October 1915. Then, on October 27, she began to break up.

Seawater rushed into the ship. *Endurance's* timbers began to break. Creaking and crashing noises rang through the ship. The crew started pumps to keep her afloat while they abandoned ship.

Shackleton knew *Endurance* was doomed. He emptied the ship of food and equipment. Shackleton said to his men, "Ship and stores have gone, so now we'll go home."

---

expand: to get bigger
timber: a long, heavy piece of wood
afloat: floating on water
abandon: to leave behind

Ocean Camp

Shackleton's crew and expedition members unloaded three tons (2.7 metric tons) of food and equipment. This included three lifeboats. They put up tents in a circle on the ice. From the timbers of *Endurance*, they made a galley and storehouse.

They called their new home "Ocean Camp." From there the men set out on many hunting trips. They hunted seals and penguins to feed themselves and the dogs.

galley: a small kitchen, often aboard ship or in camp

She's Going!

The end came for the good ship *Endurance* on November 21, 1915. Shackleton was nearby when he saw the ship move. "She's going, boys!" he shouted. All the crew hurried out of their tents to watch.

The men at Ocean Camp

Endurance Sinks

The stern of the ship rose out of the water. With her smashed rudder and propeller showing, the shattered *Endurance* sank slowly into a pool of black water. The crew stood silently as they watched her disappear.

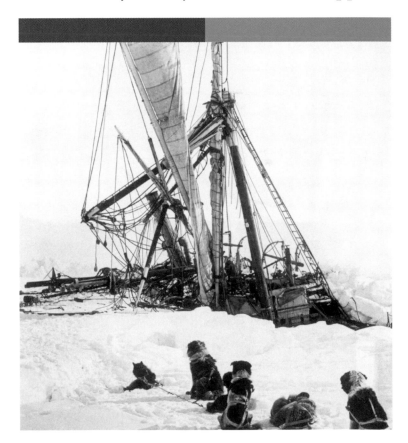

stern: the rear of a ship
rudder: a flat board which turns side to side to steer a ship
propeller: blades which spin in the water to move a ship

Cracks in the Ice

When the ship sank, the ice floe underneath Ocean Camp started to break up, too. A crack in the ice ran through the middle of camp. The men moved their camp to a safer place. All this moving made the crew weary and unhappy.

On the March

The navigator tried to chart their course. He judged that the drifting ice floe would float near Paulet Island. That was 300 miles (483 kilometers) away. Shackleton told the men to march across the ice floe. He wanted them on the side that would pass nearest the island.

The team marched at night. That was when colder temperatures froze the ice solid. The dogs pulled the supplies. The men hauled the three lifeboats on sleds.

In the floes, ice pressure builds up. This pressure bends the ice into hills. These hills proved too steep for the men to drag the boats. The march had to stop.

---

weary: very tired
chart: to determine a location using a map or other tool

Patience Camp

Shackleton and his men made a new camp.
They called this camp "Patience Camp."
From here they could still see Ocean Camp.

They stayed at Patience Camp for 14
weeks. Rations ran low. The men hunted
and ate seals and penguins. They boiled,
fried, or ate raw the meat from these
animals, including the blubber from
the seals.

Shackleton Plans a Voyage

The ice floe drifted steadily north. But it
did not pass close to Paulet Island. Instead,
the ice floe took them near land south of
the island. However, between the floe and
land lay sea and broken ice. This would be
too dangerous to cross.

Shackleton saw they would have to sail
the three lifeboats in another direction.
They would head for Elephant Island,
some 100 miles (161 kilometers) north.

---

ration: a measured amount of food
blubber: the fatty skin layers of an animal

Alone on the Ice

When *Endurance* sank, the men felt alone. Now they had to face leaving the ice floe. They would have to launch their lifeboats into the icy seas. It was the only way left to save themselves.

Escape would take all the experience and courage Shackleton and his men could muster. How would you feel if you were one of these men?

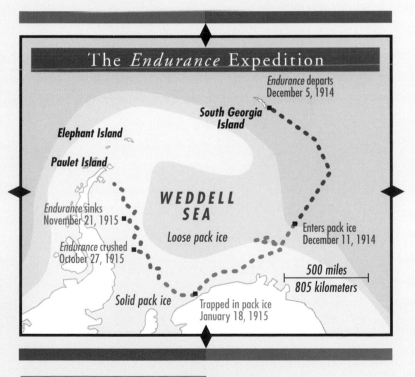

The *Endurance* Expedition

Endurance departs
December 5, 1914

South Georgia
Island

Elephant Island

Paulet Island

Endurance sinks
November 21, 1915

WEDDELL
SEA

Loose pack ice

Enters pack ice
December 11, 1914

Endurance crushed
October 27, 1915

500 miles
805 kilometers

Solid pack ice

Trapped in pack ice
January 18, 1915

---

muster: to gather or assemble

— CHAPTER **3** —

Adrift

*Frank Hurley and Shackleton
at Patience Camp*

It has been more than four months since Endurance sank. Shackleton's weary team has survived on the ice so far. Now they must take to the boats. But what will they do at night? Icy seas are dangerous to float on at night. What would you do?

No Rudder or Sail

"Our drifting home had no rudder to guide it, no sail to give it speed," Shackleton wrote in his diary. The ice floe, their "home," drifted away from land. Shackleton decided to launch the boats and escape before it was too late.

The saddest day was when they shot the cat and the sled dogs. The dogs had worked so hard for the men. They had become good pets, too. But the small boats could not carry 28 men, 69 dogs, and a cat.

Leonard Hussey with Samson, the biggest of the dogs

Man the Lifeboats!

On April 9, 1916, the men got ready to sail. Shackleton and 12 other men were in the lifeboat *James Caird*. Captain Frank Worsley took nine men in the *Dudley Docker*. Officers Hubert Hudson and Thomas Crean took the rest of the men in the *Stancomb Wills*.

When they set off, it was nearly dark. Icebergs filled the frigid sea. They soon decided it was too dangerous to sail at night. They found another ice floe and dragged the boats onto it to wait for morning.

frigid: very cold

A Man Nearly Dies

Shackleton felt uneasy on the ice floe. He walked around the camp. Suddenly, a crack appeared across the ice. It ran under the main tent. Fireman Ernest Holness fell in the icy water but was quickly pulled out. The crack in the ice closed seconds later. Holness could have been crushed and killed.

Dragging James Caird on the ice floe

Journey into the Night

Each night, after fighting the sea all day, the men rebuilt camp on a different ice floe. Each night, the ice would crack again. The men decided they must stay off the floes. They must journey by boat through the night and the deadly icebergs.

Rough Seas

The men set the sails, swung out the oars, and steered the boats for Elephant Island. They took only essential supplies. On the rough sea, spray splashed over the boats. Ice began to form on the boats' hulls in the frigid air. The men had to chip the ice off to keep the boats from sinking.

---

essential: something you can't live without

Thirsty Work

The crew had not taken enough water with them. They soon ran out. The men were painfully thirsty and cold to the bone. Then just before dark, five days after leaving Patience Camp, they saw Elephant Island.

The next morning, the men saw waves crashing on a reef. Beyond the reef was a beach. As *Stancomb Wills* was the lightest boat, they took it through the risky reef first.

Elephant Island

reef: a line of rocks under shallow water close to land

Landing on Elephant Island

Land at Last!

Stancomb Wills made it through a narrow gap in the rocky reef. Soon, the lifeboat landed on the stony beach. The stowaway, Percy Blackborrow, was the first to set foot on shore. Soon, all three boats were ashore.

For the first time in many months, the men stood on land. Used to the rolling sea, they stumbled and staggered as they walked on solid ground. They all drank water from a fresh stream. Then, they killed two seals. The cook set up his stove and they ate seal meat. Everyone felt better, happy to be on dry land at last.

Unsafe Beach

The next morning, Shackleton and Frank Hurley walked along the beach looking for shelter. Steep cliffs backed the beach. There was no protection from the wind and sea. Shackleton saw that high tide would put this beach underwater. They could not stay here. He sent Frank Wild and a few men to search for a better camping place.

The men unload James Caird, Dudley Docker, and Stancomb Wills at Elephant Island.

---

tide: the regular rise and fall of the ocean's surface

Shackleton Gets His Men to Safety

Wild returned with good news. Seven miles to the west was a spit of land that the sea did not cover—even at high tide. The next day, April 17, all three boats set off. They steered west, into the teeth of a gale. The waves and wind broke some oars, but eventually they rowed to safety.

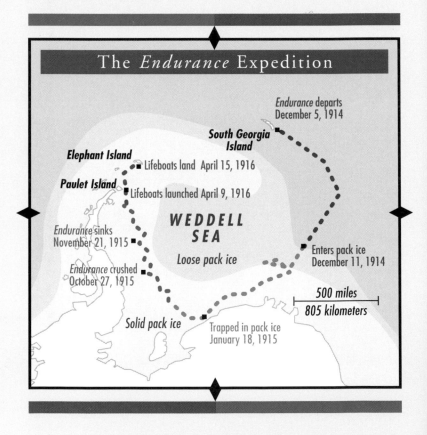

The *Endurance* Expedition

Endurance departs
December 5, 1914

**South Georgia
Island**

Elephant Island
■ Lifeboats land April 15, 1916

Paulet Island
■ Lifeboats launched April 9, 1916

Endurance sinks
November 21, 1915 ■

**WEDDELL
SEA**

Loose pack ice

Enters pack ice
December 11, 1914

Endurance crushed
October 27, 1915

500 miles
805 kilometers

Solid pack ice

Trapped in pack ice
January 18, 1915

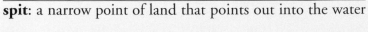

spit: a narrow point of land that points out into the water

Now What?

Shackleton had kept all his crew alive. They had all managed to get to safety. But frozen Elephant Island was uninhabited. Ships rarely passed there. What will they do now? What would you do?

Skinning penguins on Elephant Island

uninhabited: not lived in by humans

— CHAPTER **4** —

Rescue Party

There is only one hope for the crew to survive. Someone must go for help. Shackleton prepares one lifeboat for a risky journey back to South Georgia Island. How should he choose which men will go with him?

No Time to Waste

Shackleton decided to go for help. Together with five men, he would sail for South Georgia Island. He hoped to return with help in a month.

Wild would take command of the men left behind on Elephant Island. Many were growing very weak. There was no time to waste.

Shackleton had wanted to travel to Port Stanley in the Falkland Islands. That island was only 540 miles (869 kilometers) away. But the ocean winds did not blow toward Port Stanley. So Shackleton had to sail to South Georgia Island. It was 800 miles (1,287 kilometers) away.

Launching James Caird for the rescue journey to South Georgia Island

The *James Caird* Rescue Mission

Traveling with Shackleton were Worsley and Crean. Joining them were Able Seamen Timothy McCarthy and John Vincent, and Harry McNeish, the carpenter. All were expert sailors and tough, strong men.

James Caird was the heaviest and strongest boat. McNeish made a shelter on the boat to protect the men. They packed the boat with supplies. Among the supplies were two barrels of fresh water. They did not know it, but one barrel was cracked. This barrel later filled with salt water.

The men tie a barrel of drinking water to James Caird.

Supplies Taken on *James Caird*

30 boxes matches
6.5 gallons paraffin
1 can wood alcohol
10 boxes flamers
1 box blue lights
2 Primus stoves + spares
1 aluminum cook pot
6 sleeping bags
Candles and blubber oil

Food

3 cases rations
2 cases nut food
2 cases biscuits
1 case lump sugar
30 packets dried milk
1 can beef extract cubes
1 can salt
36 gallons water
112 pounds rice

James Caird set sail on April 24, 1916. The men left behind on Elephant Island waved. They gave three cheers to the departing rescue team. Their lives depended on the rescue party's success.

A Gigantic Wave

The winds were with the little boat, but gales troubled them all the way. The cold men grew weak from lack of sleep. Everything was wet. Ice built up on the boat. They were surrounded by huge seas.

At midnight on May 5, Shackleton manned the tiller. He saw a strip of pale light coming up behind them. He knew it couldn't be the dawn. He stared hard. It was a gigantic wave! Shackleton shouted to his men, "For God's sake, hold on! It's got us."

The massive wave lifted *James Caird* and flung it forward like a cork. Swirling water and sea spray covered the tiny boat. The giant wave swept past them. Water filled half the boat. Still, it stayed afloat.

The wave had passed. But now they discovered the water in one barrel was salty. The men couldn't last much longer without fresh water.

---

tiller: a long handle joined to the rudder used to steer a boat
fling: to throw hard; hurl

Land Ho!

Finally, on May 8, 1916, the men sighted South Georgia Island. It took two more days before they could land the boat. They were on the edge of King Haakon Bay.

When the men tried to drag the boat ashore, their legs and arms nearly gave out. They made camp in a cave. There they rested, ate, and drank to regain their strength.

South Georgia Island

So Close, Yet So Far

The group still had far to go. The whaling station at Husvik was on the other side of the island. Leaving the other three behind, Shackleton, Worsley, and Crean set out on foot. They took only what they could carry.

The three men climbed over glaciers. They waded through freezing waterfalls. They scaled several mountains. On one mountain top, they barely escaped a blizzard. At each crest, they hoped to see Husvik and the whaling station.

glacier: a large body of ice
scale: to climb

At last they climbed a ridge and looked out over their final goal. Far below, a little steamer entered a bay. The men could see harbor buildings and people walking around. Only a few difficult miles remained.

Eventually, after wading through waist-deep, freezing streams, the three scruffy figures stumbled into the port on May 20. It had taken them 36 hours to walk across the island. But they had made it.

Whaling station, Husvik

---

steamer: a ship driven by steam engine
scruffy: messy

Strange Men

Some small boys fled when they saw Shackleton, Worsley, and Crean. A man at the wharf fetched the manager, Mr. Sorlle. Sorlle then looked after the exhausted men. He offered them food, baths, and warm beds. At last, there was hope for the men left behind on Elephant Island.

The very next day, Worsley boarded a small ship. He sailed round the island to rescue McCarthy, McNeish, and Vincent. When the three saw Worsley, they didn't recognize him. He was clean-shaven and wore new clothes!

An Invisible Guide

Later, Shackleton, Worsley, and Crean discussed their 36-hour march across South Georgia Island. Worsley said to Shackleton: "Boss, I had a curious feeling on the march that there was another person with us."

---

wharf: a place where ships and boats can load and unload

Waiting on Elephant Island

Shackleton and his five companions had made the first part of the rescue journey. Now they had to rescue the 22 men waiting on Elephant Island. Would the ice pack prevent them getting near? Were the men still alive?

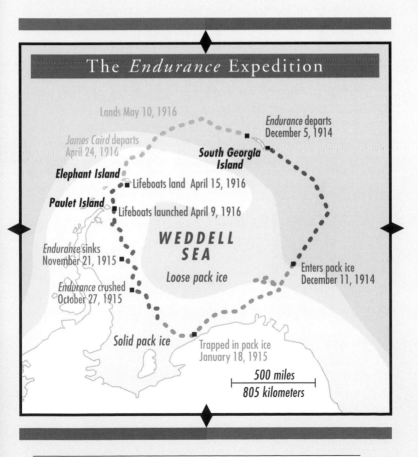

The *Endurance* Expedition

Lands May 10, 1916

James Caird departs April 24, 1916

Endurance departs December 5, 1914

South Georgia Island

Elephant Island

Lifeboats land April 15, 1916

Paulet Island

Lifeboats launched April 9, 1916

WEDDELL SEA

Endurance sinks November 21, 1915

Loose pack ice

Enters pack ice December 11, 1914

Endurance crushed October 27, 1915

Solid pack ice

Trapped in pack ice January 18, 1915

500 miles
805 kilometers

---

companion: a person who spends time with another

— CHAPTER **5** —

Survivors

Back on Elephant Island, the 22 men had no way to know if Shackleton had made it to South Georgia Island. Could Wild and the rest of the men last long enough to be rescued? Would there be enough food? Would they give up hope for Shackleton's return?

Keeping Hope Alive

Some of the men on Elephant Island were near despair. They thought the rescue team had failed to reach South Georgia Island.

But Wild was certain Shackleton would return. He worked hard to keep his men's hopes alive. Some mornings, Wild would pack up all his gear and say, "Maybe the boss will come today." He wanted to prove that he still had faith in Shackleton.

The men wait on Elephant Island for the return of Shackleton and the rescue party.

Life on Elephant Island

It was cold and miserable on Elephant Island. The men made a shelter using their two boats. They put old tent cloth around the boats to keep out the cold winds. Inside they rigged the stove. At times, blizzards covered the camp with snow. They dug themselves out each time.

Weeks and weeks passed. Wild and the men picked shellfish from the rocks. They cooked seaweed to eat. Their main diet was penguin.

Every few weeks they caught a seal. The animal's blubber made oil for the stove. The stove filled the boat shelter with thick smoke. The men and their clothes were dirtier than ever. They had no other clothes to wear. Water was too valuable for anything but drinking. Besides, it was too cold to wash.

The men used the remaining two boats to make a hut. This shelter helped the men survive the cold.

A Day to Remember

The men spent four months on Elephant Island. At lunchtime on August 30, 1916, Wild was cooking a soup of seal meat, limpets, and seaweed. Suddenly George Marston shouted from the beach, "Ship-O!"

All the men rushed to the water's edge, knocking the soup pot over, their lunch forgotten. A ship was steaming past! Wild's men lit a fire to make a signal. On board the ship, Worsley spotted the camp's fire signal.

limpet: a shellfish which sticks to rocks

The Boss Returns

Wild and his men on Elephant Island saw the ship turn toward the coast. It must have spotted them! After a while, a boat was lowered from the ship. As the boat got closer, Wild could see someone he knew. It was Shackleton himself!

When the boat landed and they saw each other, Shackleton asked Wild, "Are you all well?" Wild answered, "We are all well, Boss." The rescued men gave three cheers. The expedition was saved.

The survivors on Elephant Island cheer the rescue boat.

Shackleton took the men back to Punta Arenas in Chile, the nearest port. The whole town came out to welcome the explorers. Shackleton and his men next sailed up to Valparaiso, Chile. There every small boat in the area turned out to meet them. More than 30,000 people lined the city streets.

Life Goes On

Unlike their ship, the men from *Endurance* had endured. Thankful to be safe, they returned to the "real" world.

But it was a real world at war. World War I was under way. The men had no time to adjust. Some of the men immediately joined the war. Hurley became a war photographer. Alfred Cheetham and McCarthy were both killed in action.

Many of the men survived the war. One of them, James Wordie, became an Antarctic expert. He taught at St. John's College at Cambridge University, in England.

---

endure: to survive a hardship

Miraculous

Elephant Island could have held 22 graves. The sea or a glacier might have held six more. Yet Shackleton saved all 27 of his men. For all of them, it was a miraculous escape from an icy death.

Shackleton's expedition was well planned, well manned, and well equipped. But the weather stopped it in its tracks. The Imperial Trans-Antarctic Expedition failed to cross the Antarctic.

Yet 28 men survived the coldest, harshest conditions we can imagine. The story of *Endurance* is a story of survival against all odds. It is a story about making success out of failure. In his book *South*, Shackleton wrote:

"In memories we were rich….We had seen God in His splendours, heard the text that Nature renders. We had reached the naked soul of man."

---

miraculous: like a miracle; an extremely unusual event

Epilogue

Sir Ernest Shackleton died in 1922 from a heart attack. He was on board his ship *Quest*, beginning another exploration south.

The last surviving member of Shackleton's expedition was First Officer Lionel Greenstreet. He died in 1979.

No one crossed the Antarctic until Vivian Ernest Fuchs and Edmund Percival Hillary in 1957-1958. No one explored Elephant Island until the early 1970s. Nothing is left there to show how 22 men survived for four months in 1916.

Frank Hurley

Official photographer Frank Hurley made the expedition photographs that we look at today. In 1914, photographers needed heavy equipment to take pictures. Hurley had a darkroom on board *Endurance*. There he developed his pictures.

Some of Hurley's pictures were heavy glass plate photographs. After *Endurance* sank, Shackleton ordered Hurley to select his best photos and smash the other plates. Shackleton knew that otherwise Hurley would risk his own life to save all the photos. Hurley carried these glass plates and cameras with him on the lifeboats and to Elephant Island.

Frostbite

Many men on *Endurance* had frostbite. This is a serious condition. Extreme cold stops blood flow to fingers, toes, and other parts of the body. The flesh actually dies. The fingers or toes must be amputated.

Blackborrow, the stowaway, had to have the toes amputated from one foot because of frostbite. He got better but afterward walked with a stick.

Icebergs

Only one-tenth of an iceberg sticks out of the water. The other nine-tenths lurk under the water. So every iceberg you see is really 10 times bigger than it looks.

Icebergs are formed when glaciers break up and fall into the sea. Icebergs are huge. Icebergs have caused many shipwrecks. The most famous such shipwreck happened in 1912. That year, *Titanic* struck an iceberg and sank.

---

amputate: to cut off someone's arm, leg, finger, etc., usually because of damage or disease

Third Time Lucky

It took Shackleton three times and three ships to reach Elephant Island from South Georgia Island. The first ship made it halfway there. This steam ship could have made it to Elephant Island. But it would have run out of coal on the way back. Shackleton had to turn back.

The next ship, a wooden sailing ship, was beaten back by gales. Finally, Shackleton took a small steamer, borrowed from the Chilean government. Called *Yelcho*, this ship made it through the ice to Elephant Island. *Yelcho* then carried the rescued men safely back to port.

The Yelcho

Time Line

1914

August 8 *Endurance* sails from Plymouth, England for South Georgia Island.

December 5 *Endurance* leaves South Georgia Island for Antarctica.

1915

January 18 *Endurance* trapped in ice on the Weddell Sea.

January to October *Endurance* drifts, unable to break free from the ice.

October 27 Crushed by ice, *Endurance* begins to break up.

November 21 *Endurance* sinks.

December 29 Patience Camp set up.

1916

April 9 Shackleton and his men launch three lifeboats for Elephant Island.

April 15 Three lifeboats and 28 men land on Elephant Island.

April 24 Shackleton and five men sail in lifeboat *James Caird* to get help.

May 10 *James Caird* lands on South Georgia Island.

May 20 Rescue party reaches Husvik whaling station.

August 30 Shackleton and five shipmates arrive with *Yelcho* at Elephant Island. They rescue the remaining 22 men.

Glossary

abandon: to leave behind

afloat: floating on water

amputate: to cut off someone's arm, leg, finger, etc., usually because of damage or disease

berth: a place where a boat is tied up

blizzard: a severe snowstorm

blubber: the fatty skin layers of an animal

bow: the front of a ship

chart: to determine a location using a map or other tool

companion: a person who spends time with another

continent: any of the seven great land masses on Earth

embrace: a hug

endure: to survive a hardship

essential: something you can't live without

expand: to get bigger

expedition: a group making a long trip for a special purpose

fathom: a unit of measure; 1 fathom = 6 feet or 1.8 meters

fling: to throw hard; hurl

floe: a floating island of ice

forecastle: the front part of a ship's upper deck

frigid: very cold

gale: a strong wind

galley: a small kitchen, often aboard ship or in camp

glacier: a large body of ice

hull: the frame or body of a ship

iceberg: a large mass of ice floating in a sea

igloo: a house made of ice

limpet: a shellfish which sticks to rocks

miraculous: like a miracle; an extremely unusual event

muster: to gather or assemble

navigate: to follow a course or direction using a map, compass, stars, or other tools

pack ice: large, floating pieces of ice frozen together

peril: danger

propeller: blades which spin in the water to move a ship

ration: a measured amount of food

reef: a line of rocks under shallow water close to land

rudder: a flat board which turns side to side to steer a ship

scale: to climb

scruffy: messy

sounding: a measurement of depth

spit: a narrow point of land that points out into the water

steamer: a ship driven by steam engine

stern: the rear of a ship

stowaway: one who hides on a ship to ride for free

tide: the regular rise and fall of the ocean's surface

tiller: a long handle joined to the rudder used to steer a boat

timber: a long, heavy piece of wood

uninhabited: not lived in by humans

wardroom: the officers' lounge

weary: very tired

wharf: a place where ships and boats can load and unload

Bibliography

Alexander, Caroline. *The Endurance: Shackleton's Legendary Antarctic Expedition.* New York: Knopf, 1998.

Armstrong, Jennifer. *Shipwreck at the Bottom of the World: The Extraordinary True Story of Shackleton and the Endurance.* New York: Crown Publishers, 1998.

Hooper, Meredith. *The Endurance: Shackleton's Perilous Expedition in Antarctica.* New York: Abbeville Press, Inc., 2001.

Kostyal, K.M. *Trial by Ice: A Photobiography of Sir Ernest Shackleton.* Washington, D.C.: National Geographic Society, 1999.

Saffer, Barbara. *Polar Exploration Adventures.* Mankato, Minn.: Capstone Press, 2001.

Useful Addresses

Byrd Polar Research Center
The Ohio State University
1090 Carmack Road, Scott Hall, Room 108
Columbus, OH 43210-1002

Royal Canadian Geographical Society
39 McArthur Avenue
Ottawa, ON, Canada K1L 8L7

Scott Polar Research Institute
University of Cambridge
Lensfield Road
Cambridge, England CB2 1ER

Internet Sites

Discoverers Web
http://www.win.tue.nl~engels/discovery/

National Geographic.com
http://www.nationalgeographic.com/

Shackleton's Antarctic Odyssey-NOVA
http://www.pbs.org/wgbh/nova/shackleton/

American Museum of Natural History-Shackleton
http://www.amnh.org/exhibitions/shackleton/

Index

Antarctica, 5, 8

crew and expedition members, 7

dogloos, 11

dogs, 6, 11, 23, 27

Dudley Docker, 28

Elephant Island, 24, 30, 31, 35, 37, 39, 44, 45, 46, 47,
48, 50, 51, 53, 54, 55, 57

hull, 17

Hurley, Frank, 7, 33, 52, 55

Husvik, 42

iceberg, 8, 56

ice floe, 13, 23, 24, 25, 28, 29, 30

James Caird, 28, 38, 39, 40

Maps

Enters pack ice, 9

Trapped by ice, 14

Endurance sinks, 25

Lifeboats launched, 34

James Caird lands, 45

Ocean Camp, 20, 23, 24

pack ice, 8, 10

Patience Camp, 24, 31

Paulet Island, 23, 24

South Georgia Island, 8, 10, 36, 37, 41, 44, 46, 47, 57

Stancomb Wills, 28, 31, 32

Weddell Sea, 5, 8, 10, 12

Wild, Frank, 7, 33, 34, 46, 47, 49, 50, 51

Worsley, Frank, 7, 28, 38, 42, 44, 50

Yelcho, 57